Q&A

Darwin
...off the record

Q&A

Darwin
...off the record

PETER J. BOWLER

Foreword by
RICHARD DAWKINS

WATKINS PUBLISHING
LONDON

Darwin
Peter J. Bowler

This edition first published in the United Kingdom and Ireland in 2010
by Watkins Publishing, an imprint of Duncan Baird Publishers Ltd
Sixth Floor, Castle House
75–76 Wells Street, London W1T 3QH

Conceived, created and designed by Duncan Baird Publishers

Managing Editors: Gill Paul and Peggy Vance
Co-ordinating Editor: James Hodgson
Editor: Kirty Topiwala
Managing Designer: Clare Thorpe

British Library Cataloguing-in-Publication Data:
A CIP record for this book is available from the British Library
ISBN: 978-1-907486-61-6
10 9 8 7 6 5 4 3 2 1
Typeset in Dante MT and Baskerville BT
Printed in Shanghai by Imago

Publisher's note:
The interviews in this book are purely fictional, while having a solid
basis in biographical fact. They take place between a fictionalized
Charles Darwin and an imaginary interviewer.

CONTENTS

FOREWORD by Richard Dawkins

If we were visited by superior creatures from another star system – they would have to be superior if they were to get here at all – what would they make of the legacy of Darwin as opposed to say Marx or Einstein? Would our guests revere another Darwin as one of their greatest thinkers of all time?

When I read Darwin, I am continually astonished at how modern he sounds. Considering how wrong he was on the all-important topic of genetics, he showed an uncanny gift for getting almost everything else right. His achievement, like Einstein's, is universal and timeless, whereas that of Marx is parochial and ephemeral. That Darwin's question is universal, wherever there is life, is surely undeniable. The feature of living matter that most demands explanation is that it is almost unimaginably complicated in directions that convey a powerful illusion of deliberate design.

Darwin's question, or rather the most fundamental and important of Darwin's many questions, is: How could such complicated "design" come into being? All living creatures, everywhere in the universe and at any time in history, provoke this question. It is less obvious that Darwin's *answer* to the riddle – cumulative evolution by non-random survival of random hereditary changes – is universal. It is at first sight conceivable that Darwin's answer might be valid only parochially, only for the kind of life that happens to exist in our own little clearing in the universal forest. My view, for which I have argued elsewhere, is that the general form of Darwin's answer is not merely incidentally true of our kind of life but almost certainly true of all life, everywhere in the universe. Here, let me for the moment make the more modest claim that, at the very least, Darwin's bid for immortality is closer to the Einstein end of the spectrum than to the Marx end. Darwinism really matters in the universe.

INTRODUCTION

Darwin is one of the most controversial scientists of all time. He proposed an interlocking set of new approaches to the study of how the world we live in has come to assume its present form. His 1859 book *On the Origin of Species* persuaded scientists that they had to take seriously the claim that all living things have evolved by natural causes from previously existing types. Moreover, Darwin argued that there is no preconceived direction of development built into the history of life, and to drive home the point he proposed the mechanism of natural selection, in which populations change according to trial and error. Trivial, undirected variations are tested against the environment, and those that confer no adaptive advantage are winnowed out. Life is a never-ending process of struggle in which only those best fitted to the local conditions survive and breed.

Many people found these suggestions hard to accept, and many still reject them today. The theory renders the Genesis story of creation, and indeed the whole idea of a wise and benevolent Designer, obsolete. There seems to be no room here for the immortal soul or transcendent moral values – humans are just animals, albeit highly intelligent and highly social ones. Some religious thinkers have reconciled themselves to the basic idea of evolution by supposing that there is a divine purpose built into the process. But that is exactly what natural selection seems to deny. Materialists and atheists welcome this liberation from the shackles of ancient superstition, but some religious believers accuse Darwin of teaching us to behave like animals and thereby undermining the moral foundations of society.

Yet Darwin doesn't fit the conventional image of a revolutionary. After a voyage around the world he settled down to study pigeons, barnacles, plants and earthworms. A devoted family man, he suffered from a chronic illness and never engaged in public debates. He became a revolutionary because he committed himself to working out the implications of the theory he built on these empirical observations. He would not turn aside when it became clear that traditional ideas about creation and human nature were being threatened. We are still living with – and arguing about – the consequences of that commitment. In the following conversations we shall see how Darwin himself viewed his life and achievements.

CHARLES DARWIN (1809–1882)

His Life in Short

Charles Darwin died on 19 April 1882 and was buried a week later in Westminster Abbey. The family wanted a private funeral, but the scientific establishment wanted to honour him as a symbol of the growing power of science within contemporary culture. He had revolutionized the life sciences and changed the way almost everyone thought about the world and about human nature. A great public funeral would focus the world's attention not just on Darwin but on science itself. Sir John Lubbock (who combined the careers of scientist and banker and invented the bank holiday) arranged the event, along with Thomas Henry Huxley and other scientists who had led the campaign to promote Darwin's theory. The funeral was a grand affair, with Lubbock, Huxley and other noted figures as pall-bearers.

It was symbolic of a major transition in public attitudes that Darwin should be buried in the Abbey. Here was a man who had abandoned Christianity and had been pilloried as the originator of a theory that undermined all religious faith. Yet twenty years after the debate sparked by *On the Origin of Species*, he was honoured in death by the élites of both the scientific community and the social establishment of the time. How could a man who had been so vilified – and is still vilified by modern creationists – have gained this degree of recognition?

Darwin's achievement has been defined by two very different innovations. He convinced everyone that evolution is the best explanation of how new forms of life appeared. But he also suggested a theory to explain *how* evolution worked, a theory that seemed to deny any sense of purpose in nature. Natural selection was so radical a suggestion that most of his contemporaries did not accept it. They preferred to believe that evolution progressed steadily upward towards the human race. Darwin was buried as a hero of discovery because his theory had been sanitized to make it acceptable to the public.

Even today, most people still think of evolution as a progressive, purposeful process. But in the Darwinian system, evolution is not a ladder of progress leading up to humans. It's a branching tree of which the human species is just the tip of one branch. The process that drives the branches apart is natural selection, which picks out just those few individuals that have changed (we would say mutated) in a way that gives them an advantage in dealing with a new environment. All the rest are eliminated in a ruthless struggle for existence.

Natural selection was not the kind of process one could imagine a wise and benevolent God establishing to create new species, and conservative Christians still objected on the grounds that the immortal soul could not have evolved from the mentality of "the brutes that perish". But by the time Darwin published *On the Origin of Species* the idea of progressive evolution was not an entirely shocking idea and attitudes were changing among the more liberal components of the middle class. In the 1790s Darwin's own grandfather, Erasmus Darwin, had supported the transmutation of species (what we now call evolution) in his book *Zoonomia*. The French biologist J.B. Lamarck became notorious for suggesting the same idea. In 1844 the Edinburgh publisher Robert Chambers created a sensation with his evolutionary epic *Vestiges of the Natural History of Creation*. Although condemned by conservatives, the book was widely discussed by scientists, clergymen and the reading public, and by the 1850s the basic idea of evolution began to seem much less threatening to those with more liberal views. The middle classes wanted an ideology of social progress, so the idea that nature has produced the human race through progressive evolution seemed perfectly reasonable.

Darwin himself tapped into this ideology of progress in the closing passages of *On the Origin of Species*. But his theory of *how* evolution works was controversial precisely because it eliminated the idea of a purposeful goal. In fact it was only in the 20th century, after being linked to the new science of genetics, that natural selection became the dominant theory of evolutionary biology. Darwin is celebrated (and condemned) today both as the founder of evolutionism and as the originator of the most powerful explanation of how evolution occurs. But in assessing his life we must bear in mind that he died knowing that he had been only partially successful in getting his evolutionary programme accepted.

———

Charles Robert Darwin was born on 12 February 1809 in Shrewsbury. His father was Robert Waring Darwin. Like his own father Erasmus Darwin, Robert was a wealthy and respected medical doctor, and he also became very active in the financial affairs of the district. He married Susanna Wedgwood, whose father Josiah owned the successful pottery business of that name. Charles was the fifth of their six children, but his mother died when he was only eight and he was raised by his older sisters.

After an undistinguished school career Darwin was sent to study medicine at Edinburgh University. He hated it, especially the scenes he witnessed in the operating theatre, and soon decided that he could not continue the family tradition in medicine. He became interested in natural history, though, and joined the local naturalists' society. Here he met the radical anatomist Robert Grant, notorious as one of the few scientists who openly supported Lamarck's theory of evolution.

On leaving Edinburgh Darwin went up to Christ's College, Cambridge, to study for a BA degree, the traditional entry to a career as an Anglican clergyman. Although his father was a sceptic, the young Darwin's letters (and his later reminiscences) suggest that at this point he still had a naïve but sincere belief in the Christian message. He continued to collect natural history specimens, especially beetles. But he also took up less serious outdoor pursuits, including shooting, and his father complained that he was wasting most of his time. In fact, Darwin's scientific interests were deepening, and he gained an extracurricular scientific training that made him determined to make his mark in this area. He worked with the professor of geology Adam Sedgwick and the professor of botany John Stevens Henslow. It was Henslow who put Darwin's name forward for what was to become the turning point in his life: the voyage around the world aboard HMS *Beagle*.

Darwin had read the works of the great travelling scientist Alexander von Humboldt and had conceived a strong desire to travel to the tropics. The *Beagle* was being sent out by the Admiralty to chart the coast of South America, her second voyage to the region. Her captain Robert FitzRoy wanted a gentleman naturalist on board for company, Henslow suggested Darwin, and despite resistance from his father he was accepted for the post. The *Beagle* set sail on 27 December 1831 and was away for five years. Darwin was often free to take extended trips inland. He explored the open plains of the pampas and climbed in the Andes mountains. After casting off from the shores of South America across the Pacific, the ship moored off the Galápagos Islands for just over a month. Here, Darwin made some of his most crucial observations.

Darwin did a great deal of geological work and after his return would make his name primarily through publications on this subject. Henslow gave Darwin the first volume of Charles Lyell's *Principles of Geology*, which argued that all changes to the Earth's surface result from the action of observable causes over vast periods of time. Darwin saw evidence suggesting that the Andes had been elevated by a whole series of movements, not by a single catastrophic upheaval, thus confirming Lyell's arguments. He now wanted to explain all of the Earth's surface features in terms of gradual elevation or depression.

Lyell's "uniformitarianism" provided a model for natural evolution in the living world. Darwin was gathering information on fossils and the geographical distribution of species that would force him to reconsider his belief that each species was created by a wise and benevolent God. At Cambridge he had read a classic exposition of this creationist argument, William Paley's *Natural Theology*. Paley argued that the adaptation of each species' structure to its needs could only be explained in terms of what is nowadays called "intelligent design". But Darwin's experiences in South America forced him to rethink this argument. He saw that South America had a distinctive fauna – animals such as the armadillo and sloth. He found fossils that showed similarities to these distinctive living species. If structures are designed according to their needs, then why should South America have species that were so different from those of Africa, even though they had a similar range of environments? There were clear relationships between the successive species in each location – historical connections that could be explained by some form of transmutation or evolution.

It was in the Galápagos Islands that Darwin saw the clearest example of this process. Here was a group of islands hundreds of miles out in the Pacific. Darwin explored several of them, collecting samples of the unique wildlife. Even now, he almost missed the significance of what he was seeing. In the last few days before the *Beagle* left, he realized that there were different forms of some species on the different islands. But he had not recorded the exact locations where his specimens had been collected, and there was no time to revisit all the islands. As the ship sailed away, Darwin had to borrow specimens that had been collected by other members of the crew (who *had* noted the particular islands from which they came) to reconstruct the distribution of what are now widely known as "Darwin's finches". Each island had its own characteristic form of the birds, each adapted to a different lifestyle. Darwin became convinced that the related forms must have evolved separately from small populations derived from an ancestral South American type, pushed over towards the islands by storm winds.

Darwin returned to England in 1836 and began to write up his account of the voyage, and to arrange for the publication of his scientific observations and collections. He joined the Geological Society of

London and served as its secretary for several years. He now began to think of marriage, and proposed to his cousin, Emma Wedgwood. The couple lived in London for a short time after they wed in 1839 but then moved to a large house in the village of Downe, about fifteen miles to the southeast. Here Darwin settled down to the life of a country gentleman. The family home, Down House (now open to the public as a museum), was large and had ample grounds. His father had provided enough money to make him independently wealthy, and Darwin proved adept at making lucrative investments. At this time, however, he began to show the first symptoms of an illness which would dog him for the rest of his life, forcing him to give up active life in the London scientific community. Even so, he was never a recluse. He visited libraries and museums in the capital, received visitors at home, and built up a vast network of correspondence.

The illness may have been caused by nervous stress, because behind the scenes he was now working seriously on the "species question". Convinced that species could gradually adapt themselves to new environments, he set out to look for a cause. He investigated the one area where change could actually be observed within species – the work of animal breeders such as pigeon fanciers. In the investigations recorded in his notebooks (since published) he recognized that an important component in the breeders' success was selection. They looked for minute differences between the individuals born in each generation, and bred only from those that showed some variation in the direction they needed. Reading Thomas Malthus's *Essay on the Principle of Population*, Darwin noted the suggestion that in primitive societies the pressure of population would lead to a "struggle for existence" in which the weakest would be eliminated. Here was the driving force for a process of *natural* selection. In a changed environment, those individuals born with a slight variation adapting them to the new conditions would survive and breed, transferring their advantages to the next generation. The less fit would be eliminated. Over many generations, natural selection could create a new species adapted to the changed conditions.

In 1842 Darwin wrote out a brief description of the theory, followed in 1844 by a substantial "Essay" that could be published if he died unexpectedly. He also thought about the implications of the theory for the human species. He had seen the natives of Tierra del Fuego, at the tip of South America, considered by many to be the most "primitive" people in the world. What would it mean if the whole human race had evolved from such primitives, and they from an even earlier, ape-like ancestor? Darwin became convinced that the human mind had evolved as the highest product of a continuous sequence of mental development within the animal kingdom. Our moral values are merely the rationalization of instincts built into us by evolution so that we can live in social groups.

The 1844 Essay remained unpublished, and a variety of possible reasons can be cited for this delay. Perhaps Darwin was concerned about the public reaction, or affected by his wife's distress at his increasing scepticism about Christianity. He was also busy publishing on other topics. Most important of all, he needed more evidence that would force scientists to take evolution seriously. So Darwin continued working on the geographical distribution of species, debating with experts such as Joseph Hooker and Asa Gray whether the existing locations of species could be explained in terms of migration from a single point of origin. He undertook a major study of the barnacles, beginning with some unusual species collected on the *Beagle* voyage but eventually extending to a description of every known living and fossil species in the whole group. This project established his reputation as a biologist, but it also allowed him to investigate the range of variation within species and the bizarre adaptations that natural selection could sometimes produce.

At the same time family life continued, interrupted only by Darwin's regular bouts of illness. Several children were born and raised, although his favourite, Annie, died of fever in 1851 at the age of ten. Darwin was devastated by this loss, which may have driven the final nail into the coffin of his belief in a personal God (although he was never a complete atheist). In the mid-1850s he began to write a multi-volume account of his theory for eventual publication. This project was interrupted in 1858 by the arrival of a letter from Alfred Russel Wallace, a little-known naturalist on a collecting expedition in the East Indies, outlining a theory similar to his own. Darwin immediately thought that he had been scooped – although there were significant differences between his ideas and Wallace's – and turned to Lyell and Hooker for advice. They urged him to submit Wallace's paper to the Linnean Society for publication, along with descriptions of the theory that Darwin himself had written earlier. These included a short extract from the 1844 Essay and a letter written to the American botanist Asa Gray in 1857, making it clear that Darwin had been working on the theory for years. In the meantime he rushed to produce the single-volume account we now know as *On the Origin of Species*.

When the book appeared at the end of 1859, it provoked, as Darwin feared, a huge controversy.

Conservatives thought that it undermined faith in a God who designed the world and in the immortality of the soul. Young radicals such as the biologist Thomas Henry Huxley rushed to its defence, seeing the theory as an opportunity to free science from the influence of the Church. Darwin was not involved in the great public debates – he avoided crowded meetings at the best of times. But he was determined to defend his ideas in print, and did so through revisions of the *Origin* and by writing more books exploring aspects of the theory in detail. By the late 1860s the debate over evolution was dying down and the Darwinists (as they now called themselves) had won the day. Huxley and other scientists began a great project to reconstruct the development of life on Earth using fossils and, where they were lacking, anatomical and embryological evidence. Darwin himself did not participate in this research – he knew that the fossil record was imperfect and doubted there would ever be enough evidence to work out the details.

He brought out his own ideas on human origins in his *Descent of Man* in 1871. He accepted Huxley's demonstration that we are closely related to the great apes but was well aware that the fossil links were missing. Most other authorities at the time focused on how the human brain had become enlarged, but

Darwin suggested that our ancestors first separated from the apes by adopting an upright posture. Here, as in many other areas, he anticipated discoveries that would not be made until long after his death.

The *Descent of Man* also explored how our social instincts had evolved. Darwin argued that all species that live in social groups must develop behaviour patterns that allow for cooperation within the group. Since the groups themselves compete with one another, those in which the individuals do not pull together effectively will be eliminated. He also tried to explain how the various human races had diverged from a common ancestor. As humans had spread around the globe, isolated populations had developed their own unique characteristics. His own preferred explanation of how this had happened was sexual selection. The emergence of preferences for certain features in sexual partners had led to these features becoming enhanced in the race because parents possessing them had produced more offspring. The book upset the conservatives, but cemented Darwin's status as the architect of a theory in which competition was the driving force of progress.

Darwin was less successful in defending the theory of natural selection. Everyone thought that the struggle for existence was important, but no one could imagine that it produced beneficial results merely by weeding out the unfit. Even Huxley found it hard to believe that so haphazard a mechanism could explain the way that species evolved. The philosopher Herbert Spencer preferred Lamarck's theory in which characteristics acquired through effort and exercise are transmitted to the offspring. Although he coined the memorable phrase "survival of the fittest", Spencer thought that struggle not only eliminated the unfit, as Darwin supposed, but stimulated species to improve themselves. Other objections to the selection theory were based on the problem of heredity. Darwin provided his own theory of heredity in his *Variation of Animals and Plants under Domestication* in 1868, but he did not anticipate the concept of the gene, and the debate over how variant characteristics are inherited did little to clear the air. It was only after 1900, some twenty years after Darwin's death, that the new science of genetics provided a firmer foundation for the selection theory.

Darwin's best work in the later part of his career was in the area of botany, where he studied the structure of flowers and the activities of climbing plants. He showed how natural selection could produce structures that were hard to understand, even if you believed that they had been designed by God. His last book was on earthworms, and it was a minor bestseller among the gardening fraternity. Here is the last great irony of Darwin's life: the man hailed as the architect of a new world-view explaining how humans had evolved by struggle and progress had ended up more interested in the minutiae of adaptation and the activities of the humble earthworm. His ideas had taken on a life of their own and were being used in ways that he had never anticipated. When he died, the burial in Westminster Abbey reflected the iconic status he had gained as a symbol of the Victorians' faith in progress. He himself had preferred to cultivate his garden.

Q&A

NOW LET'S START TALKING ...

Over the following pages, Charles Darwin engages
in an imaginary conversation covering eleven themes,
responding freely to searching questions.

The questions are in italic type;
Darwin's answers are in roman type.

A RELUCTANT
REVOLUTIONARY

Darwin's theory may have had radical implications, but in his personal life he was a model of Victorian upper middle-class respectability. He was born into a wealthy family with close ties to the industrial entrepreneurs who were transforming Britain's economy in the Industrial Revolution. He lived the life of a country gentleman, raised a large family, doted on his children, and was endlessly cosseted through his periods of ill health by his wife. Although he could often work only a few hours a day, this was the perfect environment for him to pursue his studies in natural history and his writing career.

Good morning, Mr Darwin. I hope you're feeling well?

Very well indeed, thank you. I seem to have been brought back to life without all the ailments that plagued me for most of the time I was alive. I haven't felt better since I was riding with the gauchos during my explorations in South America.

You haven't always enjoyed such good health, I understand?

Indeed not. I had always suffered from occasional heart palpitations, but a few years after I returned from the *Beagle* voyage these became worse, and were accompanied by headaches, nausea and frequent vomiting. The doctors seemed to have very little idea about the causes. The only thing that worked, at least some of the time, was the water cure.

What did that involve?

One went to a hydropathic establishment such as Dr James Gully's in the Malvern hills, where they subject you to cold baths and wrap you up in wet cloths for hours. It is supposed to cleanse the system of whatever is causing the trouble. It did seem to do me some good from time to time.

It sounds as though both the illness and the cure must have interfered with your work to a considerable extent.

Of course. I could often work for just a few hours a day, so I just had to persevere with my projects over long periods of time. "It's dogged as does it," as I used to say. I couldn't stand any kind of excitement, which is why I had to give up my public life in the scientific community.

Surely you were not out of touch with other naturalists?

No – indeed to some extent I had the best of both worlds. I didn't have to waste my time on meetings and committees, but we lived close enough to London for me to visit libraries and museums when I had to. It was also easy for my many naturalist friends to visit us when we needed to talk. I corresponded with a large number of experts at home and abroad – our mail service had become very efficient by that time – and I could test my ideas against their knowledge and experience.

But you still had to adjust your life to the illness, didn't you? Can I ask about your home and family life?

I depended completely on my darling wife, Emma. She nursed me during the bad spells and ensured that I was as comfortable as possible when I was in a fit state to work. We had a very quiet life, I suppose, because although our house at Downe was only sixteen miles from London, it was real English countryside. I would work for a few hours at a time and then take a stroll around what we called the Sand Walk – a path through the woods on my small estate. Emma and I would play backgammon for relaxation, and I would listen to her playing the piano. We became quite a large family – we had ten children in all, although two of them did not survive infancy.

Obviously you were pretty well off.

Yes. I was lucky enough to be financially independent throughout my life. My father was a wealthy man and settled a considerable sum on us when we were married. I was careful with money and always made wise investments. We did very well out of railway shares. I used to keep track of every penny we earned or spent – not a bad discipline for someone who saw every living creature as keeping a kind of profit-and-loss account with nature on which its life depended.

Why didn't you try to get a professional position as a scientist?

With my poor health I could never have made a career as a professional scientist – not that there were many paying jobs in the field in any case. My friend Thomas Huxley was chained to a treadmill of teaching and government commissions throughout his life. We had to take up a collection to give him a holiday at one point when he collapsed from nervous exhaustion. I was a naturalist because I enjoyed trying to explain the diversity of life. I certainly wanted to make my mark on the world, but I didn't have to earn a living from my work.

You mention your father's wealth. Where did this come from?

Well, we were quite a prosperous family. My grandfather, Erasmus Darwin, had been an eminent doctor – he was even asked to become physician to the King at one point. My father continued in the same profession, but he also became heavily involved in the business world of the Shrewsbury district where we lived. We were closely related to the Wedgwoods, whose pottery firm had revolutionized the whole industry. My Uncle Josh – his real name was Josiah Wedgwood – was an important influence on my life, and, of course, Emma was a Wedgwood too. She was actually my cousin – I didn't have to look very far when I decided that I should look for someone suitable to marry.

You didn't mention your mother.

She died when I was only eight, and I don't really remember much about her. I was raised by my older sisters. It was a happy enough childhood, although I have to say I was not particularly good at school.

FROM HIS FATHER'S SHADOW

Darwin's early academic career was undistinguished. Having abandoned his efforts to train for the medical profession, he took an Arts degree at Cambridge, originally intending to be a clergyman. He was still not very studious, and his father began to think he would waste his whole life on idle pursuits. But outside the curriculum he was gaining experience in geology and natural history, and he now conceived the ambition of becoming a serious naturalist (the term "scientist" had only just been coined and was not yet in common use).

Would you mind telling us a little about your early career?

After school I was sent to study medicine in Edinburgh.
But I hated it, especially the horrors of the operating
theatre – this was long before the use of anaesthetics
in surgery. Eventually I had to tell my father that there
was no prospect of my becoming a doctor.

The time wasn't wasted completely, though,
because I developed my interests in natural history.
I did a lot of collecting on the sea shore and became
quite interested in the lowest kinds of animals. Some
people were already thinking of them as a kind of
bridge between the plants and the animals. This was
the view of Robert Grant, who openly supported
transmutation. I didn't pay much attention at the time.

*Yet you were interested in just those creatures that seemed
to provide a link between the two kingdoms – perhaps
Grant had at least some indirect influence on your ideas.*

I suppose that's right, although I never followed his
more radical speculations. In any case, I left Edinburgh
after two years. It was decided that I should get a
degree from Cambridge and then take holy orders.
As a country vicar I could still take an interest in
natural history.

An odd choice of career, I'd say, for someone who would later be reviled as the author of a theory that helped to undermine religion. You had to subscribe to the 39 articles of the Church of England to get into Cambridge in those days – were you able to do this with a clear conscience?

Yes, at least after some reflection. My father was not a believer, but I had been brought up by my sisters who were far more religious, and at the time I still thought that the basic message of Christianity was true. Cambridge turned out to be a wonderful place for me to go, although it wasn't the academic work that engaged me. To be frank, I had a good time – I took up shooting and other outdoor activities and got in with a sporting set of men. My father complained that I was wasting my time and would come to no good. But I was still collecting specimens – especially beetles – and had begun to learn more about natural history. I got to know Adam Sedgwick very well. He was the professor of geology and taught me how to make sense of the succession of strata in the geological record. We went on an expedition to Wales together. He was a deeply religious man and was very upset about my later ideas. But at the time he made great efforts to turn me into a competent geologist.

He didn't make any suggestion that the rock strata were laid down in Noah's flood?

Good Lord, no. The last serious geologist who actually took the flood at face value was William Buckland at Oxford. He published a book on it just before I went to Edinburgh. But even he thought the flood was responsible only for a few recent deposits. How can anyone who has done any fieldwork think that all the strata were laid down at once? There are places where the older rocks have been folded and faulted before the younger ones were laid down on top of them, and many cases of massive intrusions by molten rock within the sedimentary strata.

I only wish everyone was aware of that today, because creationism has mounted a resurgence in recent years … but please carry on with your reminiscences of Cambridge.

I also came under the influence of John Henslow, the professor of botany. It was he who put my name forward to Robert FitzRoy, who was looking for someone to travel with him when he set off in the *Beagle*. My father wasn't at all happy about this – it seemed to him a waste of time. It was my Uncle

Josh who convinced him that it would help to make my name as a naturalist.

I get the impression that you had a rather strained relationship with your father.

No, that's not the case at all. He was a very large man physically and he always seemed to dominate any conversation. But although he often chided me as a youth, we became very close later on. He was enormously supportive once the voyage of the *Beagle* was decided on. Remember I had no official position on the ship, and had to pay my own way for the whole five years. I mentioned earlier that he set Emma and me up in comfort when we got married. I owed him a great deal and it became important for me to show him that I could make a success of my work in science, whatever his earlier misgivings.

Can I ask about your wider beliefs at the time? Did you still believe that all species had been created by God?

Yes, I still accepted the idea of design. At Cambridge I'd read William Paley's *Natural Theology*, which based its argument on a simple analogy. A watch must have a watchmaker, so the far more complex structures of living things also require an intelligent designer who must be God the Creator. And since most of those structures adapt the species to its way of life, we can be sure that the Creator is both wise and benevolent. I took this on faith, although the fossil record showed that there would have to have been a whole series of slightly different creations stretching over a long period of time. The idea of design shaped my later thinking – I always accepted that the key problem if one were to get rid of miracles would be to explain the appearance of design without there being an intelligent agent directly involved.

THE VOYAGE OF THE *BEAGLE*

The great adventure of Darwin's life was his voyage round the world aboard HMS *Beagle*. It was this voyage, as he later said, that marked a turning point in his career, providing him with the basis for all his ideas. This gave him new insights into geological change and the age of the Earth. It also revealed a host of puzzling facts about the distribution of animals around the globe. His beliefs about the stability of species were undermined by his discoveries in the Galápagos Islands. Darwin's theory was founded on a new era of geographical exploration made possible by the expansion of European powers across the world.

Earlier, you mentioned Robert FitzRoy, the captain
of HMS Beagle. *What can you tell me about your*
relationship with him?

FitzRoy came from an aristocratic background, very
different from my own family's quite recent rise to
wealth and respectability. He could be very autocratic,
but he was anxious to have someone on board whom
he could talk to outside the rules of naval etiquette.
We fell out occasionally, but always made it up in the
end. One problem was his support for slavery. Like my
whole family I was passionately opposed to slavery and
saw all the races as part of a common human family.
At the time I thought that even savages were capable
of improvement. FitzRoy agreed, but he thought that
slaves were being given a better life while working for
their masters. I knew how little truth there was in that
– I saw them subjected to fearful punishments when
I was travelling in the country around Rio de Janeiro.
    FitzRoy did support the missionaries' efforts to
educate the natives in various parts of the world. He
had brought back three from Tierra del Fuego, a
desolate island at the tip of South America, when the
Beagle had called there on her previous voyage, and
had them educated to behave like English men and
women before we took them back to their homeland.

We were devastated when they soon reverted to savagery. This made me only too aware of how thin the veneer of civilization is, even with us Europeans.

Can you tell me about the exploratory trips you made?

The *Beagle* would sometimes spend months surveying the same stretch of coast, so I could spend extended periods ashore. I was very keen to explore in the tropics. I'd read Alexander von Humboldt's accounts of his explorations in South and Central America, perhaps the most impressive record of scientific observations and measurements in remote places. When we got to Bahia in Brazil I was in my element. The lush vegetation and the exotic sights were just what I was hoping for and I wanted to start collecting specimens as soon as possible. Over the next few years I was able to make several extensive trips into the interior, collecting animals, plants, fossils and minerals, and making geological observations. I rode with the gauchos on the pampas, camping with them every night. There I discovered what turned out to be a new species of the flightless bird, the rhea. We spent some time off the coast of Tierra del Fuego, where the natives we had on board were returned. And while the ship was sailing up the Pacific coast I had the opportunity to climb in the Andes.

Geology was an important part of the project, wasn't it?

Most certainly. I had been well trained by Sedgwick
and was able to make original studies of the various
rock formations. He taught me the "catastrophist"
theory according to which mountains were raised
by violent upheavals and valleys carved out by tidal
waves. But Henslow gave me a copy of Charles Lyell's
Principles of Geology, which argued that we didn't
need to invoke huge catastrophes if we imagined
ordinary causes such as earthquakes and erosion by
rivers operating over vast periods of time. This is
what is called "uniformitarianism". I saw for myself
that the Andes had been raised in stages, and that the
process was still going on. There was an earthquake
at Concepción in Chile just before we arrived. We
saw that the quake hadn't just shaken the earth – the
whole area had been raised ten feet above its original
level and you could still see where the original shore
line had been. Climbing in the Andes I saw evidence
of what were once beaches – pebbles, shells and all
– at various elevations up the mountainsides. The
entire range has been raised by a long succession of
earthquakes similar to the one we'd experienced.

I saw that Lyell was right to suppose that the Earth was immensely ancient and that all the changes affecting it had been slow and comparatively gradual.

I understand that it was by applying Lyell's theory that you developed your theory of coral reefs?

Yes, I realized then that by supposing an equally slow depression of the sea bed out in the Pacific, one could explain coral reefs and atolls. The coral animal can only live in very shallow water around the islands, so any sudden depression would kill them off. But if the sinking occurs slowly enough, they can keep building up towards the surface and will eventually ring the whole island with a coral lagoon.

The animals and plants you collected were important too, though, weren't they?

Of course, although it was only gradually that the significance of what I was seeing became apparent to me. One problem with the theory of special creation is the distribution of animals and plants around the globe. If the Creator has adapted every species to its environment, you would expect every region with the same conditions to be populated by the same species. But South America has a unique fauna quite unlike that of, say, Africa, even though it has the same range of environments. And those unique creatures – sloths, armadillos, llamas and the like – turn up in the fossils too. I called this the "law of succession of types", meaning that there is a continuity among the inhabitants of each region over time. There seems no obvious reason why the Creator would impose such a pattern, but it makes perfect sense if the later species are derived from the earlier ones.

I began to wonder why the species are located in the particular areas where we find them. I became convinced that what determines distribution is the existence of barriers preventing the dispersal of species from their original home. Mountain ranges, deserts, large rivers, all serve as barriers separating different species. The major barriers, especially the great oceans, define the main biogeographical regions on the continents. Within each region there are groups of related species, with their local distribution determined by less rigid barriers such as rivers. Every now and again species get a chance to cross these barriers and establish "colonies" in neighbouring territories. I realized that the best way of explaining the situation was to suppose that the colonists would have to adapt to the conditions of their new home.

And this is why the collecting in the Galápagos Islands became so important. But you didn't realize this while you were actually there, I believe.

Only at the very end of our stay on the islands, too late for me to make systematic collections. The islands are a terrifying place, the closest you'll find to the infernal regions on this Earth. They are volcanic and have been thrown up comparatively recently out in the midst of the Pacific. The animals are quite bizarre – marine iguanas like miniature dragons feeding off seaweed. Giant tortoises, some so big you can actually ride on their backs. It was these which gave me the clue to the strangest fact about the distribution of forms on the island. Just before we were due to leave, I learned that you could tell which island a tortoise came from by the shape of its shell. It had never occurred to me that each of these really quite small islands could have special types of its own. But we had to sail away with my collections in a muddle as far as this vital point was concerned. Fortunately, FitzRoy himself and some of the other crew members who were interested in natural history had kept better records, so I was eventually able to make sense of the situation. There were major differences between the various finches and mockingbirds on the different islands. Later on, I used the finches as a clear illustration of the situation because they show such strongly marked differences, especially in the beaks. Some had thick beaks adapted to cracking seeds, others thin ones for extracting insects from crevices, and so on.

A MOMENT
OF DISCOVERY?

The formulation of the theory of natural selection was Darwin's greatest achievement. It came through a combination of research interests which were unique to him: the biogeography of the *Beagle* voyage and a fascination with the work of animal breeders. Few naturalists were interested in the breeders' work, but they showed Darwin that there are individual differences within a population and that one can select from some characteristics at the expense of others. He also read the social philosophy of T.R. Malthus, which introduced him to the "struggle for existence". Darwin's theory would combine new ideas in science with insights derived from the more pessimistic side of Victorian capitalist ideology.

*So there was no dramatic switch in your thinking from
creation to transmutation, no "Eureka" moment, on the
islands or afterwards?*

No, it was a gradual process spread over the next few
years. We got back to England in October 1836. I
had been worrying about the Galápagos types all the
way home. Were the differences between the distinct
island populations so great as to make them separate
species? If they were just strongly marked local
varieties of a single species of finch or mockingbird,
then the creation theory would still be plausible. But
if each island type were a distinct species, then it
seemed to me that the situation would constitute a
reductio ad absurdum for creation. It's hard to imagine
the Creator performing a series of separate miracles
on each of these tiny islands out in the middle of
the Pacific. When I got home, the specimens were
sent to the eminent ornithologist John Gould for
description and classification. He assured me that they
were distinct species, not mere varieties. I became
convinced that we had to replace creation with
some form of transmutation based on geographical
isolation and the adaptation of populations to new
conditions. The ancestral finches and mockingbirds
had lived on the American mainland, and small

numbers must have been accidentally blown across the ocean by storms and had established themselves on the separate islands. Because they would not normally cross the intervening waters, each population was effectively isolated and had adapted to its new home in a different way.

So, shortly after the return from the Beagle *voyage, you became a convinced transmutationist – an evolutionist in our terminology. What was the next step?*

At this point I knew that species could change, but I wanted to know *how*. What was the actual mechanism that changed them? I spent the next two or three years gathering information on the topic and eventually came up with the theory of natural selection.

But you weren't doing this in public, so to speak? It wasn't part of your activities in the London scientific community at the time.

That's right. I settled down in London and began to get the results of the voyage published. My general account of our travels eventually became very popular, but there were more technical publications to be arranged. Much of my work was centred on my geological observations and theories. I became a member of the Geological Society and eventually served as its secretary. I wrote up and published a whole series of geological papers and monographs, including my book on coral reefs.

So your scientific colleagues would have thought of you more as a geologist than a naturalist. But the species question was beginning to take up your time in private, I assume. What did you think about existing ideas on the topic, such as Lamarck's theory?

I could never take Lamarck very seriously. His basic idea that characteristics acquired when an individual changes its habits can be transmitted to the offspring is certainly valid to a limited extent, and I have always accepted it as part of the story. When a blacksmith builds up huge muscles through exercise, there may be a slight tendency for the change to be inherited, and if a similar process went on in all the members of an animal population, the species would gradually change. But Lamarck embedded this idea in a lot of nonsense about the animals willing the new characteristic to appear. He was also convinced that there was a progressive force pushing the development of life in a particular direction, a sort of ladder of evolution the animal kingdom has to climb.

You didn't accept the idea of a ladder of progress, then?

The ladder is not a good model to use. The key process isn't an advance in a fixed direction but a more open-ended affair driven by the necessity for separate populations to adapt to their local conditions. What this produces is a branching tree with species moving apart in different directions – there can be no single goal.

I wanted to know what adapted species to their local environment, especially in cases where a population had been established in a new location. Think of the Galápagos species, which must have begun from small populations of mainland birds transported to the islands by accident. I began reading on every aspect of the topic I could think of, jotting my insights and conclusions down in notebooks. I queried experts on various topics about issues which seemed to bear on the problem, although at first I didn't let them know what my real purpose was.

I was also determined that the theory would have to be applied to man, and I was increasingly convinced that we would have to adopt a materialist viewpoint, in which the mind is just an expanded form of the mentality of the higher animals. As the size of the brain expands, so does the level of mental activity. Even our moral values will have to be explained as originating in instincts built into us by nature.

And your investigation into the work of animal breeders supported the theory?

Yes. This was one of the most important steps I made at the time. There was a huge amount of work going on in this area, both for practical purposes with cattle, sheep and the like, and by fanciers who just wanted more exotic breeds of dogs and pigeons. Most naturalists ignored the topic, because they thought the changes were "unnatural". But it seemed to me that if you wanted to understand how species change in the wild, it would be useful to study the one area where we can actually see changes taking place before our very eyes. The breeders showed me that there is variation within each species. They are alert to every minute variation appearing in the offspring of the animals they work with. These individual peculiarities are usually hereditary, in the sense that they are passed on, to some extent, to the next generation.

So a breeder picks out those individuals who have
the characteristic he is looking for, even to a slight
extent, and breeds only from those. This process of
artificial selection can produce substantial changes
over a relatively short period of time. But could there
be a natural equivalent? Was there a process in nature
that could select out a particular characteristic even
though there was no intelligence guiding the choice?

In your autobiography you laid great stress on the
importance of artificial selection, but modern historians
who have studied your notebooks don't see quite so clear-
cut a sequence of steps in your thinking.

I suppose my memory may have tidied things up a bit.
I always thought of artificial selection as a very useful
way of introducing my readers to the possibility that
there might be a natural equivalent. Perhaps the real
insight into the effectiveness of selection came when
I read Thomas Malthus's *Essay on the Principle of*
Population. I may have implied in my autobiography
that this was just part of my general reading, but of
course I was deliberately searching out books that
might throw light on human nature and its origins.
Malthus was concerned about the consequences
of human population expansion, but his book also

showed me that nature must involve a huge amount of death, because there will always be more individuals born than the food-supply can support. We can choose to limit our family size, but all the other animals are driven to reproduce without check, and it's obvious that all the offspring they produce cannot survive and breed. There must be a competition for resources, a struggle for existence in which only a few can survive. My theory of natural selection arose from a recognition that if there is individual variation in the population, some of those variants will be better fitted than others to any change in the environment, and this will give them an advantage in the struggle. They will be the ones who survive and reproduce, while those with a disadvantageous variation will tend to be eliminated. By the end of 1839 I was sure that here was a mechanism which could explain how species are transformed.

Some critics have argued that your theory creates a model of nature based on the rather harsh social conditions of the free-enterprise economy. Were you aware of these parallels when you developed it?

To the extent that I depended on Malthus's work, I suppose my ideas did reflect the values of the competitive society in which we all lived at the time. It seems obvious that high levels of ability and intelligence ultimately lead to success, and successful people usually have more children who survive to maturity. But I had to apply this model to very specific questions about how animals and plants relate to their environment. In such cases the advantage is often a physical characteristic which just happens to be useful in local conditions – and those conditions are constantly changing over long periods of time. Whatever the original inspiration, the theory takes on a life of its own when you start applying it to technical problems in natural history.

PIGEONS AND BARNACLES

Historians have often asked why Darwin did not publish his theory immediately – was he worried about the public reaction, or merely waiting until he had more evidence? Whatever the reasons, he continued to work on various lines of inquiry, hoping to establish the idea on firmer foundations. He continued to work with animal breeders, and started a new project to describe and classify all the known species of barnacles. This made his name as a serious naturalist, but also threw light on the complexities of evolution. By the mid-1840s Darwin at last began to let a few close scientific friends know about his new theory.

*You made no effort to publish your theory of natural
selection when you discovered it. Can you tell me why?*

It was one thing to have the basic idea, quite another
to work out all the potential ramifications and supply
the detailed evidence it would take to convince the
scientific community. I did write out a short sketch of
the theory in 1842 and a more substantial Essay two
years later. The latter was almost fit to publish and I
left instructions in my will that someone should be
commissioned to oversee publication if I were to die.

*It sounds as though you might have been worried about the
consequences of becoming associated with so radical an
idea. After all, 1844 was the year of the great controversy
over Robert Chambers'* Vestiges of Creation, *which had
introduced people to the idea that humans might be the
product of a progressive evolutionary process.*

There was still a huge amount to do if the theory was
to be provided with a really convincing foundation.
You should also remember that I was busy with a host
of other projects not directly connected to my species
work. I have to admit that I was worried about what
people would think, if only because I realized how
painful it was for my wife Emma to see how my work

was pushing me ever further away from the religious views she took so seriously. I suppose this may have had some effect on my decision, but I also had perfectly sensible reasons for continuing my work, with a view to publishing a really detailed account of the theory when I was sure I had dealt with all the problems. Call it a rationalization, if you will, but that was how I saw the situation at the time.

By this time you had moved out of London and had settled at Down House.

Yes, Emma and I were married in January 1839 and we moved to Downe in September 1842. After a few years, I began to let a few trusted friends and contacts know about my theory. This was essential if I was going to ask them directly how their expert knowledge might bear on the various aspects of my work. The botanist Joseph Hooker was the first – his knowledge of the geographical distribution of plants was unrivalled, and I needed to convince him that my theory was plausible. Lyell too became a trusted confidant, although he had great difficulty with the theory because he could not stomach the implication that we are descended from animals. Thomas Huxley joined the circle later on.

Can you describe the kind of work you were doing to build the evidence for your theory? I understand that the humble barnacle played a major role.

There was a huge range of projects, although you're right, the barnacles were the most time-consuming. I needed to extend my knowledge of geographical distribution because this was a key line of evidence. That's why Hooker was so important to me, and I later began corresponding with the American botanist Asa Gray. I did experiments to show how different forms of life could be transported from one area to another. I immersed seeds in sea water to see how long they remained viable – this helped to show how new islands get their plants from the nearest mainland. I even studied the mud on wading birds' feet to see what seeds, eggs and minute creatures could be carried around on them.

What about the artificially bred animals you mentioned earlier?

Pigeons and other domesticated species were still important to my work. I built up close contacts with many breeders and queried them constantly about their work. To see just how wide the range of variation was among the breeds of pigeons, we measured and compared their skeletons – Down was like a charnel house at times with pigeons being boiled down for their bones.

How did you come to realize the significance of the barnacles for your work?

The barnacles came into my life almost by accident. I had brought back some unusual species from the voyage, and no one knew what to do with them. The whole group had hardy been studied at all, and it had only just been agreed that they were linked to the crustaceans rather than the molluscs (which they resemble superficially). So I described the specimens myself, and then one thing led to another and I ended up describing all the living and fossil barnacles. This involved endless dissections of specimens to understand their internal structure. The project took over my life completely for several years. I've often told the story of when one of our children went to visit a friend and asked him where his father did his barnacles, under the impression that this was what all grown-ups did! But the work was also relevant to my wider project. I learned about the bizarre adaptations that no one raised on the theory of design would expect.

Such as?

Well, for example, did you know that in some barnacle species the male is little more than a parasite within the female? I also saw that even in wild species there is variation within each population. Domesticated species may vary because of the unnatural conditions they are raised in, but now I was sure that there was some individual variation in the wild.

THE RACE FOR PUBLICATION

Eventually, in the mid-1850s, the time seemed ripe for Darwin to write up his ideas for publication. But his plans were interrupted by the arrival of a paper written by another naturalist, Alfred Russel Wallace, outlining a very similar theory. In what has become a controversial series of moves designed to establish Darwin's priority, he and his friends arranged for the publication of Wallace's paper accompanied by a short account of Darwin's own theory, including material written long before the arrival of Wallace's manuscript. In the meantime Darwin rushed to write the book-length account of his theory (still only an abstract in his mind), which was published as *On the Origin of Species*.

When did you begin to think about publishing your theory of natural selection?

By 1850 I was more confident in my ability to persuade other naturalists to take the idea seriously. Hooker had gradually come around to accepting that migration and common descent would explain many otherwise completely mysterious facts about geographical distribution. Many other naturalists were beginning to realize that it was only by accepting a role for law rather than miracle that science could hope to understand where species come from. Even those with sincere religious beliefs saw that God might shape the world through the laws He imposed on it, rather than by a series of arbitrary interventions. Lyell and Hooker begged me to put my ideas before the public, and I began to prepare a major publication.

Was this what we now know as On the Origin of Species?

Not quite. I was planning a much bigger book, probably three volumes (like Lyell's *Principles of Geology*). It would have all the details spelled out and extensive references to the technical literature.

But it didn't get published in that form.

No – the *Origin* is only an abstract of the book I
intended to write. I think everyone knows why I had
to rush into print with a much shorter version. I never
imagined that anyone else would come up with the
idea of natural selection independently, but in 1858,
quite out of the blue, I received a manuscript through
the mail from Alfred Russel Wallace outlining the
same basic idea. I realized all too late that I might lose
my priority as the discoverer.

Who was Wallace? And how had he come up with the idea?

He was in the East Indies at the time collecting
exotic specimens of animals. Like me, he had been
impressed with the geographical evidence for some
kind of link between the species living in each area.
He had pointed out such links in a paper he published
in 1855, and had I read between the lines, I might
have seen that he was getting close to some idea of
transmutation. But the actual selection theory came
to him quite suddenly while he was suffering from a
fever. He wrote it up in a short paper and sent it off
to me because he knew I was interested in the topic.
In the covering letter he asked me to arrange for

publication if I thought the idea was worthwhile. You can imagine my consternation – I had been working on the theory for twenty years, but it would look very odd if I were to issue my big book a year or two after Wallace had already spelled out the basic idea.

You were quite sure that Wallace had the same concept of selection? I've read his paper very carefully and it looks to me as though there are significant differences between what he suggested then and your theory. He doesn't see any similarity with artificial selection, for instance. Is it possible you might have panicked and given Wallace a bit too much credit?

I didn't see it that way at the time. There were certainly some differences, and Wallace never did see the point of my analogy with artificial breeding. But the similarities were too obvious, and I couldn't afford to ignore them. He later became one of the staunchest advocates of the theory, and we debated the details endlessly.

So what did you do?

Lyell and Hooker agreed that Wallace's paper had

to be published, but they both knew that I had been working on the theory for years. They insisted that I should not lose the priority of announcing the idea to someone who had only just come up with it. They suggested that we publish Wallace's paper along with a description of my own theory, written before he came up with the idea. We used a letter I had written some years earlier to Asa Gray in America.

The two papers were read to the Linnean Society later that year, but no one seemed to notice. I suspect that a small publication in a naturalists' journal was not enough to trigger a public response. I now began to write a fuller account of my work which could be fitted into a single volume and published as soon as possible. *On the Origin of Species* appeared at the very end of 1859. I hoped that the book would force people to take the theory seriously, though I knew all too well the sort of reaction I could expect from those with conservative religious views. I didn't discuss the origin of the human race, because I knew this was the most sensitive issue, although I put in a single sentence on the topic so that no one could accuse me of concealing the point. But everyone knew from the earlier debates that transmutation meant deriving our own species from the higher animals. I feared a public outcry and had one of my

nervous attacks. I went off to take the water cure
at Ilkley and waited for the reviews to come out.

*Was there a serious risk of your theory being rejected
by the scientists?*

It was touch and go for the first few years. There
were a lot of quite negative reviews and some
important scientists came out against it. Fortunately
Huxley managed to get his very positive review into
The Times, and that helped. Over the next few years,
the positive comments gradually began to outweigh
the negative ones.

*Huxley was very active in the public debates too, wasn't
he? Your illness made it impossible to participate in these,
I assume.*

I could never have borne the excitement of the
big meetings. Everyone talked about the debate
in the following year at the Oxford meeting of
the British Association for the Advancement of
Science. Apparently the bishop of Oxford, Samuel
Wilberforce, attacked the theory and Huxley
caused an outcry with a rather caustic response to
his challenge on human origins. But I heard that

it was Hooker who actually gave the more impressive speech in favour of the theory – the whole affair was by no means the triumph for Huxley implied by many later accounts.

FLIES IN THE OINTMENT

There were many objections raised against the basic idea of evolution, and even more against Darwin's own idea of natural selection. Most of these had underlying religious or philosophical motivations, but there were also serious scientific objections to be faced. Darwin and his supporters gradually managed to overcome most of the objections, at least to the general principle of evolution. But there were many problems with the theory of natural selection, especially in the areas of variation and heredity. Many scientists – often encouraged by various moral qualms – looked for alternative mechanisms of evolution such as J.B. Lamarck's theory of the inheritance of acquired characteristics.

*Before we explore the objections to your theory, there's
another point we need to clear up, which is your position
on the origin of life itself. People seem to think your
theory is meant to explain that too.*

Not at all. Natural selection presumes the existence
of creatures which reproduce themselves. I didn't
think we had any hope of explaining how the first
living things emerged with the techniques available
in my time. Indeed in the *Origin* I spoke of life being
first "breathed" into one or a few living things to
get the evolutionary process started. Hooker didn't
like me truckling to the religious conservatives by
using biblical language, but I wanted to distinguish
my theory of how life evolves from the debate
about the first origin of life. I agree that to be a
consistent materialist you have to assume that there
was a natural origin. But we had no idea how it
might work, and I didn't want my theory to be
associated with this quite separate and very difficult
question.

*We still don't have a complete explanation. But let's get
back to the question of evolution. Was it possible for
people to accept the general idea of evolution even though
they didn't like your explanation of how it worked?*

The basic idea that later forms of life have been evolved from earlier ones had been debated for some time. Lamarck and my grandfather had argued for this and had suggested it worked through the efforts made by each generation of animals to improve themselves. Chambers' *Vestiges* had argued for some form of transmutation in 1844, although he seemed to imply that God built a mysterious "law of progress" into nature. So you could be an evolutionist without committing yourself to any particular theory about how the process worked. I certainly wanted to convince naturalists that my selection theory was plausible. But the first job was to get them to accept evolution in some form or another.

I deliberately began the *Origin* with a detailed explanation of natural selection, because that was a totally new idea which offered an alternative to design by God. Whether you accepted it as adequate or not, it showed that the subject wasn't beyond the realm of natural explanation. But then I provided a series of chapters which gave the evidence for the general idea of adaptive evolution. This was where my own work on geographical distribution, along with that of Hooker, Gray and many others, was so important. I dealt with the anatomical similarities between species which allow us to classify them into

groups. These make perfect sense on the assumption
of common descent – we can group species together
because they share basic characteristics derived
from a common ancestor, overlaid with their own
individual adaptations. Embryos are also important,
because the early stages of their development in the
egg or the womb are much less likely to be disturbed
by evolution than the later more superficial ones, so
they often reveal relationships one wouldn't expect
from the adult forms. That's how the barnacles were
recognized as crustaceans, for instance.

*What about the fossils? Many people seem to think you
ought to be able to see the whole process of evolution in
the fossil record and regard gaps in the sequences of fossils
as a disproof of evolution.*

That objection seems to come up all the time,
and I wrote a whole chapter to show that it is
unreasonable. Lyell had argued years earlier that we
have no right to expect that every species will leave
fossil remains, because the circumstances in which
bones can become mineralized are quite rare. The
record is extremely imperfect and we are unlikely to
find continuous evidence of the whole evolutionary
process. There are new discoveries being made all the

time and we may occasionally find intermediates
that will show we are on the right track. But to argue
that the absence of a complete fossil record for
evolution counts against the theory is to misunderstand
the nature of the geological record.

*What about the development of the embryo? Doesn't that
show us all the details in a speeded-up form?*

Not really. What you are referring to is the
"recapitulation theory" which led some naturalists to
become overenthusiastic about the parallel between
embryological development and the evolutionary
history of the species. The confusion arose partly
because the very terms "development" and
"evolution" were originally applied to the process by
which the fertilized egg matures into an individual
organism, but were then extended to cover the
changes which take place in the overall history of life
on Earth. As I mentioned, embryos are important
because their early stages sometimes reveal affinities
between species. But that's not the same as saying
that the development of the embryo is like a speeded-
up version of evolution. The point is that evolution
is a branching process, not a linear one. You should
never fall into the trap of thinking that one species

is an "immature" form of another. Embryos are not ancestors, although they may sometimes give you clues about what the ancestors looked like.

I think this is getting us onto the thorny issue of progress. Would it be fair to say that most of the people who accepted the general idea of evolution saw it as an inherently progressive force. And where does your own theory stand on that issue?

There was a general enthusiasm for the idea of progress and a lot of rather sloppy thinking about how it might apply in the history of life on Earth. There's no doubt that there has been progress. Some modern species are far more complex and highly organized than those we find earlier in the fossil record. I always thought that natural selection would have at least some tendency to make species more efficient at what they do. But as I said earlier, there is no automatic force pushing things up a preordained scale of perfection. That's where Lamarck and Chambers went wrong. Simple organisms can stay simple as long as they are well adapted to a stable environment. In any case, evolution is a branching process, and although some of the branches may occasionally develop new and more complex

structures, there is no requirement for all of them
to do that. When species adapt to a parasitic lifestyle,
they degenerate and lose their more complex organs.
And those that do become more complex can do so
in many different ways – they are not all climbing the
same ladder. I was happy for people to see evolution
as a process that can sometimes generate progress
towards higher things – indeed I ended the *Origin*
with an appeal to precisely that sentiment. But it is
frustrating when they think this means everything
is somehow trying to become human.

*So there were many people who accepted evolution, but
not the theory of natural selection. Why do you think
there was so much opposition to that particular idea?*

Most people seem to assume that evolution must
have a purpose. It's hard for them to understand that
it doesn't, at least in the sense of a force directing
every detail. This is a particular concern for religious
believers who want to retain some idea of design
by God, but it runs even deeper than that. Natural
selection seems to violate this assumption of purpose,
and all too often this produces an almost instinctive
reaction against it. The astronomer Sir John Herschel,
whose opinions I had previously valued because

I admired his book on the scientific method, called it "the law of higgledy-piggledy". I was often criticized for basing my theory on mere "chance" because the variations within a population on which selection acts seem undirected. These variations seems "random", but of course they're not. There are causes at work that we didn't really understand in my day but, whatever they are, they produce many different variations in structure, the majority of which are not directly related to the adaptive pressures facing the species – which is why selection is needed to weed out the many useless forms. That's how each local population can adapt to its environment in its own way, as in the Galápagos.

The critics are always looking for examples of changes that could not be explained by selection. The anatomist St George Mivart – who had originally studied under Huxley – wrote a book called *The Genesis of Species* in which he listed a number of alleged cases where selection could not work. He argued that when there was a major change in the function of a structure, the intermediate stages would be useless for either purpose. If a leg is changing into a wing, for instance, as when birds evolved from reptiles, the intermediate steps would involve structures that couldn't be used for flying yet, but would no longer work properly for walking. I don't see how we can be so sure of this, myself. If the chimpanzee and gorilla were extinct, would anyone believe there were species that could function partly in the trees and partly on the ground?

I don't like to mention personal issues, but Mivart was a Roman Catholic, and his enthusiasm for attacking my theory clearly stemmed from his wider beliefs. He fell out with Huxley over this and was by no means altogether honest in his dealings with me, so he was excluded from our circle.

There was also a great deal of debate over the question of heredity. Can you explain your own views on this topic and how you related them to the selection theory?

There were many efforts to argue that on the basis of what we knew about heredity, the selection process would be ineffective. A Scots engineer, Fleeming Jenkin, wrote a telling review of the *Origin* which made me think more carefully about this issue. He pointed out that if an individual were born with a really strongly marked variation, its offspring would not have the new characteristic to the same extent because the other parent would have to be a normal individual. My own theory of heredity, which I called "pangenesis", certainly implied that if you join the reproductive materials from two different parents, the offspring would have to be a mixture of the parental characteristics. Jenkin argued that if this were the case, favourable variations would be diluted in each generation and thus render selection ineffective.

You never thought of the possibility that characteristics could be inherited as fixed units? That's how we understand heredity today. We've identified units in the chromosomes of the cell nucleus which control how particular characteristics develop in the embryo – we call them "genes". These are transmitted more or less unchanged from parent to offspring, so the characteristics themselves are inherited as units.

That seems a rather odd way of approaching the topic. I know there are a few characteristics which are inherited like that – bright blue eyes are a good example – but they are quite uncommon. If a very tall man marries a very short woman, wouldn't you expect their children to be of intermediate height? But Jenkin was wrong in any case to suppose that variants appear as single individuals, although I admit that some of my earlier descriptions might have implied this. As Wallace pointed out, it is much better to think

of a range of variation across a whole population. In
the case of humans, there are a few very tall people
and a few very short people, but most of us are
ranged on a continuous distribution in between. If
selection acts on this kind of variation – for instance,
if being taller became an advantage – then everyone
over average height would benefit and leave more
offspring. Shorter individuals would be less successful.
I'm convinced that whatever the laws of heredity turn
out to be, the process of selection can work.

*I get the impression that many people were desperate
to find something that would push evolution in a
predetermined direction. They wanted anything but
"random" variation at the mercy of the environment.*

Yes, anatomists such as Mivart were especially prone
to thinking that development must be constrained.
They didn't want to see evolution as a haphazardly
branching tree. For them it had to be being pushed
in a particular direction, and they were quite willing
to imagine parallel lines of evolution all advancing
through the same sequence of evolutionary stages.
Each line was supposed to develop towards the
same goal, defined by the most "mature" stage
of development, although they would reach it

independently of one another and possibly at different times. There was also the idea that the process came in a series of discrete steps, the theory of evolution by "saltations". Even Huxley was tempted by this – he supported my theory because he could see that it made a good stick to beat the theologians with, but he was never convinced that selection was the sole cause of evolution.

But what about adaptation?

Very few naturalists thought it was as crucial as I did, and some dismissed all adaptive characteristics as superficial. Even those who did think that most characteristics have some adaptive value seem to prefer Lamarck's explanation of how they are produced to my own theory of natural selection. This was certainly true of Herbert Spencer, who made his name as the philosopher of the evolutionary movement. He was a bit too much of a philosopher for my taste, always theorizing from first principles and inclined to ignore facts that didn't fit into his deductions. He welcomed the theory of natural selection and coined the term "survival of the fittest", which caught on as a convenient shorthand description of my theory. But he always thought

that the Lamarckian process was more important.
He imagined the animals changing their habits in
response to a new environment, with the result
that they exercised their bodies in new ways and
developed some structures at the expense of others.
For some reason the example of the giraffe stretching
its neck to reach the leaves of trees has become the
most common way of visualizing the process. The
point made by Lamarck and Spencer was that if these
individually acquired modifications are inherited by
the offspring, the process becomes cumulative over
many generations and you end up with the giraffe's
long neck. I certainly think this effect is valid, but only
as a supplement to natural selection. For Spencer
it was the other way round. The novelist Samuel
Butler also supported Lamarckism, and became
quite abusive towards me. He accused me of failing
to acknowledge that Lamarck and my grandfather,
Erasmus Darwin, had come up with the idea of
evolution long before I did. He also thought their
explanation was better than mine because it was less
materialistic.

A DANGEROUS IDEA

Natural selection was unacceptable to many because it seemed to destroy the element of purposefulness in the world. It invoked the image of a world based on chance and death. Most of the rival theories were intended to retain some role for purpose – perhaps even a divine purpose – in nature. But the basic idea of evolution also threatened other cherished assumptions, especially by implying that human beings are merely well-developed animals. The selection theory seemed to undermine the foundations of traditional morality by making selfishness the basis of all animal, and human, behaviour.

I ought to warn you that our current model of heredity doesn't allow for the Lamarckian effect, but it would take too long to explain why. Your mention of Mivart and Butler's antagonism brings us closer to the more controversial implications of your theory. Perhaps we can begin with the question of human origins, and the popular assumption that your theory implied that we're descended from apes?

In my *Descent of Man* I certainly pointed to the evidence that Huxley and others had offered to show that we are closely related to the African great apes. But it's an oversimplification to suggest that my theory implies that we're descended directly from them. Remember the point I made earlier that in a theory based on branching evolution, one modern species cannot be the ancestor of another. What "being related" means is that both are descended from a common ancestor. I've no doubt that if we ever find the fossils of the common ancestor of apes and humans, we would classify the species as an ape, but it would be a generalized ape, lacking the specialized features of the modern chimpanzee and gorilla. They have developed too, along different lines which have adapted them to their lives in the forests.

*But something special seems to have happened to our
ancestors, although you argued strongly that we are not as
distinct from the higher animals as most people imagine.*

I was convinced from the start that we would have to
treat all our supposedly distinct human characteristics
as products of the evolutionary process. We have
much higher mental powers, we have language,
we make tools, and we have moral or social values.
But these are just extensions of potentials already
existing in the higher animals, and they must have
been expanded by the normal forces of evolution,
in particular by natural selection. I made a serious
effort to show that the higher animals, at least,
show some rudiments of the mental powers and the
social instincts which we find so well developed in
ourselves. I particularly remember a story I reported
in the *Descent of Man* about a monkey at the zoo
which risked its own life to save the keeper when he
was attacked by a fierce baboon. Surely this is some
evidence of an altruistic instinct in animals.

*We tend to be a bit more careful now about stories
reported by untrained observers – they all too easily read
human abilities and values into what they see in animal
behaviour. But in any case, how do you think these*

*characteristics became so greatly enhanced in the course
of human evolution?*

A lot of people seem to have thought that getting
bigger brains and more advanced mental powers
was somehow inevitable. But when you think of
evolution as a branching process you see that it's
necessary to ask a very different kind of question.
If getting more intelligence is such a good thing,
why did the apes get "left behind"? To me it seemed
obvious that we had to think of some adaptive change
which separated our ancestors from those of the
great apes. The key transition, I'm sure, was when
our ancestors moved out of the trees and became
adapted to walking upright on the open plains of
Africa. This left their hands free for picking up sticks
and stones to use as tools, which would have provided
an incentive for them to develop a higher level
of intelligence. The apes stayed in the trees and
became ever more strongly adapted to a way of life
which limited their ability to manipulate things
with their hands.

*That's a very perceptive point, and we now have fossils
that confirm that the first hominids, as we call them,
walked upright but still had ape-like brains.*

That's exactly what I could never convince anyone of in my time. They all expected to find a "missing link" that would have a bigger brain but still lived in the trees.

Of course, this idea would undermine any hope of seeing humans as the goal of evolution – which was the one thing that reconciled people to the theory. After all, given slightly different circumstances in Africa a few million years ago, we'd still all be apes.

True enough. But the *Descent of Man* created an uproar anyway. There were still many deeply religious people who saw the essence of humanity as the product of an immortal soul somehow plugged into the physical body. Whatever your theory of how evolution works, you have to abandon that position – unless, of course, you want to give souls to animals. I had been convinced since I first started thinking about these issues in the 1830s that the mind is a product of the physical operations of the brain. If we get bigger brains, we get more highly developed mental faculties. And, of course, the whole idea of original sin goes out of the window too. This was one of the points that the bishop of Oxford urged against my theory when he attacked it at that debate in Oxford in 1860 – long before I published my detailed views on the topic. There really isn't much one can say in response to this view. It's very hard to reconcile any position in which humans have evolved from lower creatures with the old Christian view that we have fallen from a higher state.

Fortunately, there were liberal clergymen willing to compromise on this issue. Charles Kingsley, for instance, was enthusiastic about my ideas. He even talked about them at a level suitable for children in his *Water Babies*. I'm sure you've read his humorous description of the debate between Owen and Huxley over how closely we're related to apes. But he was also very clear about the importance of seeing living things as the products of a process, not a series of individual miracles. There's a very effective passage in which Tom, the water baby, talks to "Mother Carey", a personification of nature, and is amazed to find her sitting still rather than dashing around creating things. She tells him it's not necessary, as she "makes them make themselves". Pure Lamarckism along the lines peddled by Spencer, of course, but at least Kingsley saw that it was better to think of the Creator as working through nature rather than always interfering. The problem was that, at the detailed level, my theory made it much less easy to see a divine purpose in nature.

DECLINING
FAITH

Darwin was well aware that his version of evolutionism made it very difficult to believe that the world had been created by a wise and benevolent God. He believed that while nature looks as though it is designed, in fact its relative perfection is a product of trial and error. And the adaptation of structure to function is not an indication of the interest taken in the design by a benevolent Creator. The driving force of evolution is struggle, and the death of those individuals with the slightest harmful characteristic, not some purposeful directing agent. For this reason, nature shows as much evidence of cruelty and selfishness as of well-being and harmony. But there were also other, more personal factors involved in Darwin's own loss of faith.

Obviously you've thought very carefully about your views on religion. Can I ask if you feel any discomfort at the impact your ideas have had? Indeed, has anything of your own youthful faith survived?

This is an uncomfortable issue for me, in part because my dear wife Emma remained true to the Christian faith. I certainly began from that position. I explained to you earlier that in my day you had to be a practising member of the Church of England to enter Cambridge University. It was only later on that I began to realize that the world wasn't quite the nicely designed and orderly place that the advocates of natural theology claimed it to be.

You've mentioned that you started off believing in the idea of design by a benevolent God. Can you say something about how you lost that belief?

I'm well aware that there are many structures in animals and plants that look like contrivances designed by a skilled engineer. Much of my later work on the structure of flowers such as orchids was intended to show just how sophisticated some of these structures are. They certainly look as though they were designed, and I suppose I still occasionally find that way of thinking about them easy to fall into. But natural selection shows that evidence of design can't always be taken at face value. Just because something looks designed doesn't mean that it is.

How so?

Well, once you realize that there are processes of trial and error going on in nature, you see that the whole point of natural selection is that it keeps picking out the very few useful variations and getting rid of the rest. This means that, of course, structures will get more efficient as time goes on, until they reach a level of apparent perfection. Remember, though, that the adaptive value of most structures is only relative to a particular environment – if the conditions change, some other characteristic may become more advantageous and selection will start in a new direction. Sometimes that may not be possible. If the species has become very strongly committed to a particular lifestyle, it may be trapped in a dead-end from which it cannot retreat. For instance, think what would happen to giraffes if the trees on which they feed disappeared – they would find it very hard to adapt back to a less specialized form of feeding and would probably become extinct. There is also the case of parasitic lifestyles, where it may be positively advantageous to lose complex structures that are no longer needed.

What about really intricate structures such as the human eye? Can you really believe that such perfection can be built up gradually by a series of accidents?

Well, I used to be bothered about the eye, and still am occasionally. But in the case of such a useful organ, any improvement is likely to be beneficial in most environments. If you can see a whole sequence of intermediate levels of sophistication in the animals stretching from the most simple kind of eye – just a spot of light-sensitive tissue – up to our own, it's not quite so clear that the final level can't be reached via those intermediate stages through a steady process of improvement.

It's also worth remembering that, for all the claims of the natural theologians, many structures – including the human eye – aren't as perfectly adapted to their purpose as you might expect if they were really designed by a supremely intelligent Creator. We are all the products of history, and a long way short of perfection. Ask the medical doctors about that, or anyone like myself who has suffered from chronic illness all their lives.

But it wasn't just the elimination of the positive evidence for design that undermined your faith?

No, although that was certainly part of the story. To be frank, even now I still occasionally wonder if it might be possible to reconcile evolution with the vision of a Creator who set the universe going at the beginning in the hope that something worthwhile would eventually emerge within it. But that Creator certainly can't take a personal interest in every individual organism. There's too much death and suffering in the world for that, some the deliberate result of "design". Think of parasites that have evolved to get their livelihood by tormenting their hosts. Think also of Malthus's principle of population: it's inevitable that most organisms die young because there are simply too many born in every generation for the food supply to support. Whichever way you look, nature turns out to be ruthless and indifferent to the individual – all that seems to matter is gaining a temporary advantage in the "struggle for existence". I didn't make up that phrase, incidentally, it comes from Malthus, and the basic principle is valid whether or not struggle plays a positive role in allowing the fittest individuals to survive and breed. As I once told Hooker, one could write a good book for the use of a Devil's chaplain by simply describing the cruelty that we see around us in every field and hedgerow. And that's all part of the story of how the species interact in the so-called "balance of nature". In the *Origin* I used the image of an "entangled bank" to describe all the interactions between species. They are certainly all entwined, and it may all look harmonious, but it's actually a scene of constant struggle.

You mentioned your own illness just now – weren't there some more personal factors that undermined your faith?

This is very painful for me, but yes, there were personal tragedies which made it difficult for me to carry on believing in a caring God. My favourite daughter Annie died horribly at the age of ten, back in 1851. I don't think I ever recovered properly from that. How could a caring God design a world in which the innocent suffer and are snuffed out in that way?

Another very personal reason for my loss of faith was that it eventually came home to me that my father, my brother, and many of the best people I know, were damned as far as the most committed

Christians are concerned because they don't accept that Jesus Christ is the saviour. Just because they thought for themselves and decided that the evidence didn't support the Christian view of God, they are damned – even though they did their best to live a good and decent life. I can't believe in a God who requires such a rigid belief in the significance of a single historical event.

There's a story that you underwent a deathbed conversion back to the Christian faith.

Nonsense. I died as much an agnostic (to use Huxley's term) as I had been for the previous twenty years. There were several members of my family around me when I died, and if you check their reminiscences I'm sure you'll find nothing to back up that story.

SOCIAL
DARWINISM

It was easy to imagine that in a world created by natural selection only an instinct for "success at any price" would guarantee progress. Therefore to many Darwin's theory seemed to imply that the old moral values taught by Christianity would have to be abandoned. In fact, the new culture of free-enterprise capitalism, which flourished during the industrial revolution, meant that people in the West were already used to the idea that it was better to stand on their own feet. So these "new" moral values may not have been all that different from those of the old Protestant work ethic. Darwinism also threw new light on how the human races were related.

If you don't accept the Christian value system, on what do you base your own moral code? It was claimed that your theory undermined traditional morality by justifying a policy of "might is right". Nowadays they call this "social Darwinism" and blame it for some pretty horrible things that have happened since you died.

My own moral code is that of an English gentleman, and I think I upheld it pretty well. I'm certainly aware that some people in my own time made claims similar to those you mention. There was a newspaper article arguing that my theory justified Napoleon and every cheating tradesman. The philosopher Herbert Spencer seemed to think that the competitive state of the natural world made it necessary to have a competitive society – it was the only way for the human race to improve itself. I assume this is the sort of thing you mean by "social Darwinism".

That's certainly one version of it. And as we've mentioned, Spencer did coin the phrase "survival of the fittest", which you accepted as a valid description of natural selection.

That's true, but Spencer and I both recognized one important point about an evolutionary explanation of human morality. We humans are social animals and we have to cooperate with the other members of our own social group. We may want to increase our status in the group, but we can't do that in a completely ruthless manner, because if we did the group would simply disperse. Our ancestors almost certainly lived in groups too, just like most of the modern great apes.

So is it this need for cooperation that gives us our sense of morality?

Yes, in these group circumstances natural selection will give the individuals social instincts which modify selfish behaviour. I believe, as does Mr Spencer, that these cooperative instincts are the basis of our moral values. In effect, we behave decently to our fellows because we have built-in instincts to do this – and then our philosophers and religious leaders take those instincts for granted and claim they are implanted in our conscience by a God who requires us to obey them.

How does natural selection actually build up these cooperative instincts?

I think that once animals begin to live in social groups, natural selection operates at a new level. Of course, it still picks out the best individuals. But it also picks out the most successful groups, and this means that those groups in which the individuals cooperate most effectively will beat those which are more loosely organized. So cooperative instincts are actually enhanced by natural selection operating between the groups rather than between the individuals.

That idea is pretty controversial nowadays, but in any case it still makes competition the driving force. Your critics are even more concerned that the idea of the strong conquering the weak has been applied to nations and races, in effect justifying war and the extermination of unfit races.

I wish you'd make your mind up about this social Darwinism you complain about. My name seems to have been associated with anything that vaguely depends on competition. First you were linking my theory to Spencer's philosophy, which hailed free enterprise and individual competition as the driving force of progress. He opposed the idea that the state should build up a strong military force to pursue its ends. Now you seem to be accusing me of inspiring nations to take up arms against each other to prove which race is the strongest – which has nothing to do with a competitive marketplace. States which place a high value on military strength usually have tightly controlled societies which don't encourage individual initiative – exactly the opposite of a free-enterprise economy. Competition at the national level seems to stifle the freedom to compete among individual citizens. How can my theory be responsible for inspiring such incompatible policies? People just take the basic idea of struggle and apply it in whichever way suits them.

Please, Mr Darwin, I'm not accusing you of anything. I'm only reporting the charges made by others, and I agree that the term "social Darwinism" has been applied too widely. They even claim that your theory inspired the belief that the black races are inferior to the white.

I used to think that all the human races were capable of improvement. I explained my passionate hatred of slavery at the time of the *Beagle* voyage, and I have always been determined to show that all the races of mankind have descended from a common ancestor. That was certainly not what some of the slave-owners believed.

They argued that the ancestors of the black races were separately created from Adam and Eve, making them distinct species. Louis Agassiz, one of the leading American opponents of my theory, argued for this position.

Later on, I became increasingly doubtful that all the races were capable of raising themselves to the same level of civilization. They have all branched out from a primitive common ancestor, but some of the modern races have advanced further from that ancestral type than others.

In what respects?

Well, I'm not convinced that they have the same intellectual capacities as us, although I'm aware how difficult it is to judge that when they 've been so badly mistreated. Most of the anthropologists of my era had come to accept that there were differences between the intellectual capacity of the races, and I quoted some of their measurements of relative brain sizes in my *Descent of Man*.

Those figures are now widely rejected as products of prejudice and preconception. Fundamentally, the human species is surprisingly uniform – the physical differences between the races are pretty superficial. That's the view accepted by most Darwinists nowadays.

I'd certainly prefer to think that my theory was being used in that way rather than as a means of supporting the deliberate exploitation of other races. But it's very confusing to realize that my name is still being bandied around in this way. I'm still not sure that I understand who's on my side and who's against me.

A CLASH OF VIEWPOINTS

Thanks to the development of genetics, modern Darwinism bases its interpretation of evolution on the mechanism of natural selection. But Darwin himself would only be aware of the term "Darwinism" being used in the more general sense of "evolutionism". Modern creationists object to both natural selection and the general theory of evolution, in effect returning to a position popular when Darwin was a young man. Given his early experiences as a geologist, he would be amazed to find that there has been a revival of the belief that the Earth is only a few thousand years old.

All biologists working in the appropriate areas of science are now on your side, at least as far as the general importance of evolution is concerned. The theory of natural selection is still seen as central to our explanation of most areas of evolution, so biologists still call themselves "Darwinists".

So my approach was vindicated in the end – well that's nice to know, I suppose. In my later years I felt that we had given the theory of evolution a firm foundation, but support for natural selection actually seemed to be diminishing rather than increasing. People were calling themselves "Darwinians", but all they really meant was that they accepted the basic idea of evolution. But I get the impression from what you said earlier that there are still many ordinary people who reject the theory.

There has certainly been a rise in what we call fundamentalist religious belief, and this has fuelled widespread reaction against both evolutionism and the selection theory. These are the people who accuse you of precipitating a collapse of moral values.

I suppose if you rock the boat pretty violently, you have to accept that people will start to panic.

I was certainly aware that I was encouraging them
to rethink some of our most basic presuppositions
about how we fit into the natural world and how that
world operates. I have to accept some responsibility
for the various ways people have tried to work
out how to live in a world without the traditional
comforts of religion. But I was primarily a naturalist
and I always felt that one should study the world as
one found it and try to explain it as best one could.
If the world turns out to be more complex and less
comfortable than people had hoped, and they find
it difficult to live with the consequences, I can't help
that. I'd be devastated to think that they might retreat
back to the old illusions just because they can't bear
to face the consequences of thinking for themselves.
Better to accept the nature of the real world and try
to live with it as best you can.

FURTHER RESEARCH

THE VOYAGE OF THE BEAGLE

Darwin's account of the voyage of the *Beagle*, which was originally entitled *Journal of Researches into the Natural History and Geology of the Various Countries Visited by HMS Beagle*, is available in numerous modern editions.

THE ORIGIN OF THE SPECIES

This text is also widely available – most reprints are of the much revised sixth edition of 1872, but purists might prefer the first edition, available in a facsimile edition (Cambridge MA: Harvard University Press, 1959). Note that the "On" was dropped from the title of later editions.

THE DESCENT OF MAN

Less frequently reprinted, but there is a new version introduced by **James R. Moore** and **Adrian Desmond** (London: Penguin Classics, 2004).

AUTOBIOGRAPHY

Darwin's *Autobiography*, published after his death without his comments on sensitive issues, was later reprinted in full, edited by **Nora Barlow** (London: Collins, 1958).

CORRESPONDENCE

Multiple volumes of Darwin's correspondence are being published in a series by Cambridge University Press, originally edited by **Frederick Burkhardt**. Access to his works and to many of the manuscripts that have survived (including his research notebooks) is available through: www.darwin-online.org.uk.

OTHER WRITERS ON DARWIN

There have been many studies of Darwin and his influence, some by writers who dislike the theory (e.g. **Gertrude Himmelfarb**, *Darwin and the Darwinian*

Revolution, New York: W. W. Norton, 1959).

The most substantial modern biography is in two volumes: **Janet Brown**, *Charles Darwin: Voyaging* (London: Jonathan Cape, 1995) and *Charles Darwin: The Power of Place* (London: Jonathan Cape, 2002). **Adrian Desmond and James R. Moore**, *Darwin* (London: Michael Joseph, 1991) is a powerfully written account stressing the political implications of his work.

For a general introduction try **Peter J. Bowler**, *Charles Darwin: The Man and His Influence* (Oxford: Blackwell, 1990; reprinted by Cambridge University Press, 1996) or, more generally, the same author's *Evolution: The History of an Idea* (revised edition, Berkeley CA: University of California Press, 2003).

David Kohn (ed.), *The Darwinian Heritage* (Princeton NJ: Princeton University Press, 1985) is a collection of detailed pieces of Darwin scholarship.

DOWN HOUSE
Down House and its gardens (where Darwin spent the later part of his life) are open to the public. They are situated in the village of Downe, Kent, about fifteen miles to the southeast of central London.

INDEX